THE PUZZLE OF HAZEL TREE FARM

K.S. Aitken

The Puzzle of Hazel Tree Farm

Editing, Cover Design and Formatting by Let's Get Booked:
www.letsgetbooked.com

Print ISBN: 978-0-9928542-1-8

CHAPTER 1

SCHOOL'S OUT FOR SUMMER

School was over. The last chime of the bell had scarcely faded, and, caught up in the mass of bodies escaping the school, Charity Glenn was already halfway down the path, sprinting as fast as she could towards her bus. After a near stumble, she fell into the nearest seat and took a deep breath of baked summer air. She closed her eyes and relaxed, imagining the wonderful adventures she could have in the long school holidays now that her first year at secondary school was over. Until her phone vibrated. She snapped out of her pleasant dreams and sighed deeply, frowning as she fished her phone out of her pocket. She braced herself for the message. She knew what it would say...

Me and Mum in meeting. Do not disturb. Lasagne in fridge.

Dad x

Deflated, she slumped in her seat. It seemed this holiday was going to be like any other, and it hadn't even started yet. There would be none of the family trips abroad or movie marathons she'd heard so much about from her friends. It would be another dull holiday full of endless business calls and important meetings, and she wouldn't even be able to catch up with her sister Chloe because instead of coming home from university for the summer she was volunteering as a leader with the Girl Guides at the world scout jamboree in the US.

Everyone in her form was doing something exciting over the summer, even boring old Harold was going to Cornwall, and he wouldn't shut up about what a great time they'd have camping and having beach bonfires together as a family. Why did she have to have such busy parents? She understood they had to work hard at their business but sometimes she felt like they didn't care about her.

The bus came to a juddering halt. Charity hadn't even noticed that, while she had been lost in thought, they'd pulled up to her stop. She grabbed her bag and descended the steps before walking the short distance home.

***

The large and modern detached house was as pristine on the inside as it was on the outside. Floors and surfaces gleamed, cushions were plumped and unwrinkled and vases of similar but different white flowers were tastefully arranged in every room. Not a thing was out of place; not a single dust mote could be seen dancing in the sunlight spilling in through the sparkling windows: it was like a show house.

Charity kicked off her shoes, leaving them wherever they landed before trudging upstairs to her room. Inside, files, school books and magazines covered any available space. She dumped her school bag on her unmade bed and discarded her uniform on the floor, kicking it into the corner. She pulled open a drawer and took out the first things she saw, which happened to be a pair of green shorts and a crumpled grey T-shirt. Sighing she flopped onto her bed with her phone and hurriedly texted her friend Sophie.

Hi Soph. Only 10 minutes into the holiday and I'm already alone. Parents busy as usual. Can tell this is going to be an "awesome" holiday. Do you want to meet up?

She flicked through her phone and started to play *Candy Crush* while she waited for a reply. Five minutes later her phone buzzed and a text message appeared:

Hey feel sorry for you 😢 *Can't meet up, soz. I've just been told we're going to Thailand! Parents kept it a secret. Got to pack. Hope your hols get better xx*

Charity sighed and flung down her phone. It hit the bed so hard it bounced off and bungee jumped towards the floor. She scrambled to catch it before it landed but wasn't quick enough. Fortunately, its fall was broken when it landed inside one of her trainers. The way it stood bolt upright made Charity imagine a gymnast landing perfectly after a series of backflips. She almost expected it to take a bow.

Retrieving her phone out of its landing place, she stalked down to the kitchen, passing the closed door of her parents' office. She narrowed her eyes and glared at it, calling it some names to vent some of her frustration and disappointment.

Once in the kitchen, she flung open the fridge door and peered in. Shoved on top of various takeaway boxes, was a plastic container with a peeling green Post-It note stuck to it.

Lasagne. Three minutes in the microwave. Don't make a mess x

Charity sighed. No matter how many times she told her parents, they *still* didn't remember that she was a vegetarian. She'd only declared that she was turning veggie to get their attention but that, like the mess she deliberately made everywhere she went, hadn't worked. True, the mess often got her shouted at, but only in the same way that someone might shout at a cat for scratching the furniture: it was soon forgotten about.

She pictured her dad writing the note in his large, heavy handwriting. He was a burly man with a shock of red hair. He might've appeared jovial if it weren't for the severity of his pale blue eyes. It was sometimes hard to know whether he was joking or being serious. With her mum though, it was always clear. She never joked and rarely saw the funny side of things. She had jet back hair, like Charity, but that's where the resemblance ended. Charity wore her roughly brushed hair in a loose ponytail most of the time, whereas her mum scraped hers into a tight knot that showcased her hard, sour face.

It was about 9pm before her parents emerged from the office, looking worn out and dishevelled. Her mum had strands of hair sticking out of her untidy bun, looking like she'd been pulling at it and her dad's shirt was untucked and creased. They didn't bother getting changed, they just pulled some leftovers out of the fridge and slumped down on the sofa with Charity, who was watching TV.

"So, summer holidays hey?" her father balanced some rice on chop-sticks as he looked at her. "Mmmm," she replied, keeping her eyes on the screen.

Nothing could be heard but the TV for a while as her parents munched their food, then her father stretched and put his hands behind his head.

"So…" he started again. "Your mum and I have been talking," he said, glancing at his wife's stony face before turning back to his daughter. "We're going to be busy for the next month or so – we've just arranged a big deal with a client and we need to make sure we deliver what we've promised. That won't leave us much time for you, I'm afraid."

Charity scowled and continued to stare at the TV screen.

So… how would you feel about going to stay with your uncle at the farm for the summer holidays?"

Charity's eyes swivelled towards him. He looked hopeful. Like he was really counting on her saying she would go. She thought about being difficult for a moment – throwing a tantrum and saying she wouldn't go. That everybody else was going on holidays with their parents – just to make things hard for them as revenge for ignoring her – but she knew that if she refused to go, she'd have a miserable summer. She loved her uncle Henry and her aunt and cousins, and she hadn't seen them for a while. It must have been three years since she'd last stayed there. She could remember feeding the hens and the calves; the way the calves would lick her hands with their slimy, rough tongues; the sticky residue of their saliva on her fingers that she wiped off with straw. She remembered giggling with her cousin, Nora as they played hide-and-seek in the outbuildings. It was meant to be Nora's older brother who was seeking them, but it had been Skye, the dog, who'd found them crouching behind a stack of feed bags. The girls had squealed in surprise when Skye leapt over the bags and pounced on them. The dog had loved their reaction, wiggling and wagging her feathery tail in delight, while covering their faces with excited licks. Yes, it could be fun on the farm in summer. Plus, she wouldn't have to constantly worry about making any sort of mess in the farmhouse as her aunt and uncle weren't as demanding as her mother was about being tidy.

"If you want," she replied, sulkily, not wanting to let them know that she was quite pleased with this plan, and hoping to make them feel guilty.

Unfortunately, they seemed oblivious to her tone of voice and exchanged looks that showed her they were pleased to be getting rid of her.

"Go up and pack then," her mother chivvied her, "and then we can take you through first thing in the morning. Uncle Henry knows you're coming."

Oh, so it's all arranged then, Charity thought resentfully. The thought that her parents couldn't wait for her to leave stung her. They wouldn't have been packing Chloe off somewhere if she'd been here.

"AND TIDY THAT ROOM!" Her mother bellowed after her as she climbed the stairs, adding insult to injury.

CHAPTER 2

GOOSE ON THE LOOSE

Charity was supposed to have packed the night before, but the temptation of *Candy Crush* was too much and she hadn't got much done.

That morning she was awoken by her parents, up and moving about, probably eager to get rid of her. Still in her pyjamas, she chucked her ratty old trainers into her case on top of a mountain of creased clothes. Tucking a stuffed rabbit with one eye into her backpack, she wondered if she could sneak some sweets and biscuits in without anyone noticing.

Charity turned around and briefly noticed her reflection in her mirror. Her black hair was usually pulled into a ponytail, but now it fell in a long wave. *Where did I put my bobble?* she wondered, scanning the room for anything she could use to tie her hair back.

"Charity! Are you done yet?" her mum's voice echoed from the bottom of the stairs.

"Nearly," she shouted back. Charity knew she'd never get away with half the things she'd packed, so she didn't want her mum to come and inspect her bag.

"Oh, what's taking so long?"

"I'm almost done," she said quickly. But it was too late. Her mum's footsteps were already coming up the stairs.

"Charity, what are you doing?!" Her mum cried as she entered the door.

"Just packing."

"You CANNOT pack *those* trainers, or those disgusting old T-shirts." She cautiously crept over to the bed and gingerly picked up a wrinkled T-shirt, looking at it as if it were a dead rat. Then she reached into the wardrobe and pulled out a crisp new Mickey Mouse top, still with labels attached.

"Put this on. It's brand new." She nodded towards the pile of clothes. "I'm going to have to pack for you."

"*You?*" Charity asked.

"Yes *me*," she said whilst sifting through the wardrobe. "Then you won't look like you've come straight from a jumble sale. I don't understand you, Charity. I've bought you lots of nice clothes … this one, this one, this one …"

Her arms disappeared into the wardrobe whilst she mechanically passed out the clothes.

Great, Charity thought, knowing that the 'nice clothes' her mother would pack would be completely unsuitable to wear on the farm.

Two hours later Charity was miffed; crammed into the back seat along with her luggage, and a few extras smuggled beneath her coat. She sighed and turned to her breakfast, which had hurriedly been shoved in her hand as she was pushed through the door. Her parents seemed to think that she still *liked* jam sandwiches without crusts.

Rain streaked down the windows, even though yesterday had been a lovely summer's day. *It's a bad omen,* Charity prophesised.

Eventually, they turned onto the road that led to her uncle's farm. At first, Charity didn't realise where she was as the road was unrecognisable. It was strange: it used to be flanked by fields and bushy hedgerows with wild roses sprouting off the grassy verges. But now the fields had been stripped of their green carpet and were filled with sleeping JCBs, piles of breeze blocks and huge, brown muddy puddles. A sign had been erected stating:

'Coming Soon: Hazel Lodge Housing Estate: 3-4 bedrooms available'.

Charity's eyes widened in horror. *What's going on here?*

Her thoughts were interrupted when her mother took a sharp turn into the Hazel Tree Farm yard, nearly running over a goose, which honked and flapped its enormous wings indignantly as it strutted away, glaring at them. Charity was surprised to see that the usually tidy farmyard looked unloved and scruffy, with straw needing to be swept up and a quad bike that clearly needed some repairs left abandoned by the wall.

She'd expected that Uncle Henry would be out to greet her with her oldest cousin Alfie to help with the bags, but only her aunt was waiting for them, huddled against the rain.

Something must be up, Charity thought, her excitement dampening. The one thing she noticed that hadn't changed was the farm dog, Skye. She was as hyper as ever and seemed pleased to welcome them.

"Would you like a cup of tea?" her aunt, Sarah, questioned Charity's parents as they dumped her bags in the porch.

"Oh, no thank you, we're on a tight schedule," her dad said. "Best get home and get on with things. He turned towards Charity, "Well, have a great time. Text us and let us know what you're up to."

"Be good," was all her mum said as she gave her a peck on the cheek. Then they drove away leaving Charity to follow her aunt into the farmhouse.

CHAPTER 3

GWEN GLENN

As she and her aunt stepped into the farmhouse kitchen, a warmth settled over Charity like a familiar blanket. It was like coming home, rather than coming to visit. Aunt Sarah handed her a steaming mug of tea, which her chilled hands clasped gratefully; the white, rising mist tickling her chin. The contents of the mug were uncommonly copper, addressed by Aunt Sarah's apologetic cry. "Sorry, we're out of milk!" Not wanting to seem ungrateful or rude, she strained to swallow the bitter, murky liquid, pondering over how peculiar it was that a dairy farm had no milk.

Her aunt dashed off somewhere, leaving Charity alone in the kitchen, her legs swinging restlessly as she glanced around to see if there was anything to occupy her. The kitchen hadn't changed much since her last visit; the boiler was still rumbling away, the worktops were still cluttered and a collection of boots and shoes still littered the tiled floor. But now there were no games to play, books to read, not even a farming magazine flung across the table. She was disappointed to see that all the shelves were empty of everything apart from files which were bursting to the brim with paperwork.

Just as she was looking around, the kitchen door creaked. Aunt Sarah obviously hadn't closed it properly. She waited to see who it was: would it be Uncle Henry or one of her cousins coming to say hello? The door slowly swung open ... revealing no-one. Charity lowered her gaze and to her surprise, she saw a mischievous face staring back at her, as if it were saying, *what are you doing here?* Charity blinked as she took in the image in front of her: furry, horned face with wide yellow eyes and black slits for pupils. The face was absent-mindedly chewing on a man's slipper.

Charity stared at the goat.

The goat stared back.

The staring match was interrupted when a door on the other side of the room bust open and her cousin Nora bounced into the kitchen with a panicked expression on her red face.

"Have you seen Gwen?" she asked, then added helpfully, "the goat."

Charity raised an arm and pointed at the other doorway where the offending animal was still snacking on her uncle's slipper. Nora scrambled around the kitchen table, heading for the animal. Instead of turning around, the goat dashed through her legs and into the kitchen. The next few minutes spiralled into chaos with Nora scampering around after the goat, managing to bump into the stool that Charity was sitting on. About to place her mug on the table, Charity wobbled and missed, dropping the mug. It smashed on the floor, spilling its contents. Murky liquid flooded the floor adding to the pandemonium. Still the goat continued to outwit the girls. By now, Charity had joined in the mission, but every time they got close, Gwen slipped past like butter.

“What's all the noise?” came a voice from the doorway. It was Rowan, her ten-year-old cousin. His spiked red hair made him look like a shocked hedgehog. The way he stood in the doorway, feet planted firmly, hands on hips, made him look like a miniature superhero. “Don’t worry. *I’ll* catch the goat!” Rowan declared, pushing out his chest.

“No, Rowan, the floor is too –” *CRASH!* “Slippery,” Nora finished looking down at her brother, face planting the tiles.

Everyone froze as Aunt Sarah came through the door, clutching bags of shopping. She gazed speechlessly at the sight that greeted her; Rowan sprawled on the floor, the two red-faced girls standing breathless by the kitchen counter, tea spilt over the tiles next to the smashed mug and the goat looking slightly bored, the slipper still dangling from her mouth as if nothing had happened. All of a sudden it scarpered through

Aunt Sarah's legs, causing her to stagger and nearly drop the shopping. Rowan and Nora belted out, chasing after it as it headed up the stairs, leaving Charity to face the music.

"Sorry about this." Charity looked at the floor. She followed it up with a rushed explanation of what had gone on in the kitchen as Aunt Sarah recovered from the shock and put some milk in the fridge.

Just then, Uncle Henry came into the room followed by a young man. Charity immediately noticed a change in her uncle. There were large bags under his eyes, as if he hadn't slept for days, and his shoulders were hunched, giving him a decidedly weary look. Charity frowned. Uncle Henry usually appeared firm and sturdy. He took one look at the state of the kitchen, turned and went upstairs without even speaking.

"Hi, Charity. Nice to see you again," the young man greeted her.

She stared. It took a while before she realised it was Alfie, her oldest cousin. "Blimey! You've grown since I've last seen you."

Alfie cracked a smile. "So have you, Tiny. Except you aren't so tiny anymore, maybe I should rethink that nickname"

"Nora!" Charity heard her youngest cousin Rowan shout from the top of the stairs, "Your stupid goat has eaten my feather boa!"

"Gwen can't help it, she's only a goat," Nora shouted back. "She doesn't understand what she's doing! Don't be so hard on her."

The shouting match came to an abrupt stop as Uncle Henry came stomping downstairs with a disgruntled looking goat under his arm. In one swift movement, he opened the back door and threw her out into the rain. She could be heard bleating as the door was slammed shut.

"But Daaaaad!" Nora moaned,

"No buts," Uncle Henry snapped. "Goats don't live in houses."

Charity, detecting an unusually strained atmosphere, decided to get out of everyone's way. She crept up the creaking stairs, took a sharp turn and entered the room that she had stayed in on her last visit. It had been cosy then, with light blue walls and a comfy bed. But the guest room was showing signs of decay and wear. Damp was creeping up the back wall and paint was flaking from around the radiator.

"Sorry about the mess," Aunt Sarah said, surprising her as she came up silently behind Charity. "We haven't had much time to prepare for your arrival. We only knew you were visiting when your parents told us yesterday.

We were going to redecorate but we've been a bit short of money recently."

"Oh?" Charity said, her voice rising to make it a question.

Her aunt plonked herself down heavily on the bed and Charity noticed that she too didn't look her usual self. Her normally soft face looked tight, as if she was clenching her teeth, and her clothes seemed baggier on her body.

"We've always done okay, earned enough to run the farm, feed the animals, look after ourselves and even go out for a nice family dinner now and again. But now ... well, we're struggling. With that awful hard winter we had followed by this hot summer, we can barely feed the animals. I'm delighted it's raining today… But don't worry, dear, I'm sure it will work itself out." Aunt Sarah smiled weakly at her. "Why don't you start to unpack? I'll be downstairs making dinner."

She heaved herself off the bed slowly and made her way back downstairs.

Charity laid her case on her bed and opened it. She fumed when she saw the contents.

"Nora! Do you have any clothes I can borrow?"

Nora appeared in the doorway. "Er … yeah, why?"

Charity looked at the disgustingly frilly items her mother had packed for her and laid out the few wearable items on her bed. Nora shook her head. "Your mum *did* know she was bringing you to a farm, didn't she?"

She left Charity staring incredulously at the clothes her mother had packed for her before returning with a pile of her T-shirts and jeans. Charity breathed a sigh of relief, shoving most of her own back into her suitcase and kicking it into a corner. It was a good job that she and

Nora were the same age and she could borrow from her.

She sat on the creaking bed and started to think about what her parents were up to. They hadn't texted to check in on her. *They're probably just working, like always,* she thought sourly.

Charity made herself useful in the house for the rest of the day, cleaning up the mess in the kitchen and doing some baking with Nora.

Eventually, the first day passed and Nora, Rowan and Charity headed up to bed. Nora hadn't had any spare pyjamas so she'd had to wear the new pyjamas that her mother had packed. The crisp, stiff cotton was chilled with that coldness that often lingers within newly bought clothes, and she longed for the warm, tatty fleece of her old onesie. The slightly musty duvet bit at her ankles, sending cold shivers down her spine as she tried to find a comfortable position. When she finally settled down, she noticed the silence – so unlike the sound of cars and the neighbours arguing that she was used to at her own house.

When she'd heard she would be spending the summer holidays at the farm, she'd been looking forward to seeing everyone again and having fun with them, but now…she got the feeling that this was going to be a summer to remember for all the wrong reasons.

CHAPTER 4

ROSES AND RAIN

Charity was woken up the next morning by a cold sensation on her shoulders. She tugged at the duvet, trying to wrestle it back up to keep herself warm, but it was torn from her body. She jolted upright and opened her eyes to see a pair of yellow orbs staring back at her.

"Goat!"

Gwen stood at the end of the bed, staring back at her, with the end of the duvet stuffed in her mouth. Charity could have sworn the mischievous goat winked at her.

"Right you!"

Outraged, she leapt out of bed and attempted to grab the goat but it swerved away easily as she chased after it. Shutting the bedroom door to prevent its escape, Charity waited until Gwen was distracted by a particularly tasty shoe and dived on top of her. The goat did not seem shocked or dismayed at finding herself pinned to the floor by a girl in pyjamas.

Charity stood up with Gwen in her arms and, surprised at the goat's weight, began stumbling awkwardly downstairs with her. Gwen didn't struggle as she had a new distraction: nibbling on Charity's hair.

"Gerroff!" She shook her head angrily to try and stop her hair from being eaten.

The front door was gaping wide open. Uncle Henry must have forgotten to close it properly when he and Alfie went out to milk the cows. No wonder Gwen had got inside. Charity quietly strode out of the house, onto the pathway and across to the old stable. Its door was also open slightly. Clearly, whoever had put Gwen away last night hadn't bolted the door properly. Charity shoved the goat in and took care to make sure the bolt was all the way across.

Turning her back on the stable, shaking out her aching arms, Charity's eyes searched the farmyard. She took in the broken bits of machinery and guttering, straw lying scattered around the yard, and paint peeling on the buildings. Everything looked a bit uncared for, not how it had been on her previous visits.

"What's going on?" she muttered before turning around and going inside.

Still in her pyjamas, which now had a suspicious brown smear on the chest, she went into the kitchen where her aunt was cooking bacon and sausage.

"Aunt Sarah?" she asked. "You know I'm vegetarian, right?"

"Are you?" Aunt Sarah whipped round from her cooking to face her. "I didn't, sorry...err, I'll put some eggs on for you."

"Thanks," Charity replied, just as Nora entered the room. Her arrival had been announced by her enthusiastic but totally tuneless singing as she came down the stairs.

"Morning!" she cried, flopping down into the seat next to Charity.

"Morning love." Aunt Sarah smiled. "I was thinking; after breakfast, could you and Charity go and feed the calves?"

"Sure."

"Charity, would you be okay with that?"

"Yeah that's fine, I'd love to help!" Charity said, excited about seeing the cute little calves.

"Good. Right. I'm going into town and Rowan's coming with me."

Rowan, who had just come into the kitchen, complained "WhydoIhavetodothat?" all in one breath.

"Because, young man, if you want to help on the farm, you need a pair of boots that fit you and don't have holes in them," his mother reminded him. "Dad and Alfie will be busy in another field, so you two will be on your own. Is that okay?"

"Yeah," both girls replied at once.

"NO!" Rowan shouted.

After breakfast, the two girls went down to the stable where the calves were kept. On the way, they saw Alfie and Henry loading some fence posts into the mud-splattered pickup truck to take to one of the fields where the fence needed repairing. Nora told Charity that this was a regular event as the field bordered a bad corner where drivers often ignored the bend sign, went too fast and ended up in the field after crashing straight through the fence. Another one must have gone through just a couple of days ago as the fence was damaged again, although, unusually there was no sign of a damaged car that needed to be dragged out by their tractor. "Costs Dad a fortune in fencing," Nora said, glancing at her father's strained face as they passed by. "He's going mad about it. It's just another thing we can't afford at the moment but it's got to be done to stop the cows getting out and causing an accident."

Charity followed Nora into the stable. She watched as Nora filled up several bottles with the special milk mixture.

"It's a bit watery. Is that how it's meant to look?" Charity asked puzzled.

Nora sighed, "we've had to change to a cheaper whey-based brand and it isn't as good as the skim-based one we usually have."

"Oh." Charity frowned, getting a sense that the farm was in real trouble. *So much for a fun-filled summer here,* she thought, sulkily. Everyone was miserable and stressed.

"Anyway, it's pretty straightforward: hold out the bottle for the calf. It'll have a sniff at first to check it out, then start sucking from it. Don't force it into its mouth, they don't like that."

She handed one to Charity and gestured towards one of the black and white calves crowding around their ankles and snuffling at the straw-covered floor. Charity fumbled the bottle towards one of the calves, who gave it a delicate snuffle, before eagerly sucking the fluid from the plastic bottle.

"Oooh look, Nora!" Charity exclaimed, almost dancing on the spot. "It's drinking it."

Her cousin smiled. "You're getting the hang of it!"

As they made their way around the crowd of calves, Charity noticed something was wrong.

"Hey, Nora? How many calves did you say there were again?"

"Fifteen, why?" Nora replied distractedly, still trying to feed one of the other calves.

"There's only fourteen," Charity quickly counted again to be sure.

"Oh no... Please don't tell me one has escaped."

Nora quickly checked the calves' ear tags and discovered that it was Milo, one of the biggest calves, who was missing.

"If he gets hurt, Dad will get really mad and I'll get all the blame. We have to find him, Charity!"

Nora frantically grabbed Charity's hand, pulling her along with her as they ran towards the corner of the field where the fence was awaiting repair. There was nothing to see and the temporary blockade didn't look to have been disturbed.

The girls looked all over the farm for the missing calf, but didn't find any sign of it. After searching everywhere, a distant mooing sound grabbed their attention, and stopping to listen, they tried to pinpoint its direction.

"Oh no! It's coming from the village. I hope it's not Mr Reekworth's garden again." Nora sounded mortified. "He hates our guts. And if we get in hot water with him, we get in hot water with Neighbourhood Watch AND the Parish Council."

"Let's go, then," Charity said. "We'd better find him."

The girls hurried back through the fields, in the direction of the nearby village.

The grass darkened under their feet as ominous clouds appeared overhead. CRASH! A distant rumble of thunder echoed around the pair.

"We'd best hurry. There's a storm coming, let's –"

"There it is again, I heard him mooing!"

The girls ran together towards the gate out of the field they had been searching and raced up the road towards the village. They knew they were on the right track as they were able to follow a trail of cowpats. It was like Hansel and Gretel following pebbles.

Soon they reached the first houses of the village. Another, louder 'moo' broke the silence of the sleepy rural atmosphere.

"Oh no," moaned Nora as she saw the cowpats heading towards the pristine garden of the nearest house. "We're doomed!"

They crept towards the garden, hoping not to be seen, when their worst fears were realised. Milo the calf was standing amid Mr Reekworth's prize-winning roses, happily chewing and trampling them to smithereens. Nora was frozen to the spot in horror, her hands covering her face. Charity stifled a chuckle at the situation and earned a death stare from Nora who was peeking through her fingers but still rooted to the spot. The sight of Milo moving towards an exquisite butter coloured rose snapped her out of her reverie. She leapt towards him, pulling a long length of baling twine from her pocket like a lasso. She looped it around the cheeky calf's neck and began to pull him away from his next snack. Milo was not keen to leave his newfound favourite delicacy and mooed moodily.

"Help me!" Nora barked at Charity who was bent over laughing helplessly. "It's NOT funny!"

Charity gave Milo a strong shove away from the roses. Reluctantly, the naughty calf gave up on the yellow rose and allowed himself to be dragged away.

"Come ON," Nora urged. "Faster, before Mr Reekworth sees what you've done."

Just as the struggle was ending and Milo was successfully extricated from the rose bed, a soft purr could be heard behind them. Nora turned and looked towards the driveway gate. Her face turned milk-white as she beheld the horrified face of Mr Reekworth peering through the windscreen of his sporty yellow BMW.

No-one moved. Even the calf seemed to know the trouble he was about to be in and hung his head guiltily. The effect was ruined slightly by a rose petal stuck to his lower lip which made him look as if he was sticking his tongue out. Charity sniggered at the sight.

Mr Reekworth opened the car door, grunting as he shuffled his walrus sized body out the driver's seat until he stood before them, the buttons of his cardigan straining as he puffed himself up even more. His small piggy eyes were wide beneath his bristly white eyebrows and his chins wobbled alarmingly as his mouth began to open in slow motion.

Nora flinched and ducked, as if the words about to come towards her were boulders. The phrase '*sticks and stones may break my bones but words can never harm me*' jumped into Charity's mind and sang to her in jaunty, mocking tones. But as Mr Reekworth's furious words were hurled towards them, she realised just how wrong that little saying was.

Just as they were being pelted by the force of Mr Reekworth's rage, the brooding clouds chose that moment to tip and spill their misery all over the ruined garden and the group within it.

Suddenly, it wasn't funny anymore.

CHAPTER 5

FUNNY BUSINESS

While Nora, Charity and the calf remained outside, Mr Reekworth had plodded back into his house with a snap of, "stay there!" He pointedly made phone calls from his front window, in full view of the mortified pair, first to Uncle Henry, then the Neighbourhood Watch and finally the Parish Council. "It's vandalism!" They heard him bellow to Uncle Henry down the phone. "I demand compensation!" There was a pause while he listened to Uncle Henry's reply. They could see his face turning beet-red and his chins wobbling furiously behind the rain-streaked window as he roared, "From your insurance!"

Trouble was, Uncle Henry didn't have insurance. It was one of the first things to go, as he couldn't pay all the premiums that came with insuring the farm.

Both girls could do nothing but stand there in the pelting rain and occasionally pull Milo away from snuffling at Mr Reekworth's only surviving patch of roses. Nora was anxiously twisting the twine that held Milo, in her hands, worried that Mr Reekworth was going to come back outside. Charity could see it all in her head now, the trouble they were going to be in and the consequences they would face.

Headlights briefly distracted the pair. Uncle Henry's muddy van had appeared, the cow trailer bouncing behind it. Though the driver couldn't be seen in the gloom, Nora tensed and muttered, "Oh, I'm really in for it now," under her breath.

The van door opened and Uncle Henry slumped out. He wore his weariness like a familiar scarf; the girls knew that it was the fatigue of all the hard work he was doing to keep the farm going.

Upon Uncle Henry's arrival, the front door opened, and Mr Reekworth hurried down the path like a penguin.

"SEE THIS!" he shouted, waving his hand at his destroyed garden. "It's ridiculous the way you let your animals and your kids run riot. What do have to say for yourself?"

Uncle Henry blanked him and instead turned to the girls.

"Put Milo in the trailer," he growled. "Then get in the car."

Nora's downcast, guilty expression only intensified at the sight of her worn-down dad, a far cry from the jovial and fun-loving father she'd always known. Nora and Charity bundled Milo into his trailer before they scrambled in and drove off, leaving Mr Reekworth behind them, screaming, "you'll pay for this!"

"I don't believe this," Uncle Henry said, breaking the silence that had engulfed the van before going back to staring at the road ahead of them.

Then... laughter. Muffled, gleeful laughter escaped from Uncle Henry, who was suddenly almost in tears from the force of it.

"I can't believe that blinking calf actually did that," he cried, slapping the steering wheel and making the girls jump suddenly. "I've had enough of that grumpy old snob with his sports cars always getting his knickers in a twist over trivial things! He's always complaining about the farm: the smells, the mud on the roads from the tractors, even 'the unsightly black wrapped bales' and the cockerel crowing. And all the while he's been breaking the hosepipe ban just so he can water his blooming garden! Honestly, that man is such a menace, I'm glad the calf wrecked his precious garden. It's like the cows' revenge."

The girls were so shocked that all they could do was look at each other, eyebrows raised and their mouths in a perfect "O" shape.

"You're not cross?" Nora asked hesitantly.

"No, of course not."

"But...he's making you pay for his garden and he's reported you to Neighbourhood Watch AND the Parish Council."

"He can't make me pay," Uncle Henry said. "And anyway, I've got more serious things to worry about. The Parish Council can't make me pay a fine! Not if they expect to use the hayfield for the village fete again."

Nora and Charity chuckled along with Uncle Henry, relief flooding over them. The ride back was full of contented silence, broken only by Uncle Henry humming an upbeat tune to himself and the girls exchanging happy looks every few minutes, giggling to themselves.

That night, Charity finally had a moment to text her parents, but stared at the blank bubble for a few minutes. Would they even respond at all, or would it be another case of waiting for hours to receive a one-line response? She contemplated not bothering but decided she had to text them - even if she didn't get a response – to let them know what was going on.

Finally, after a few minutes of thinking, she tapped away until she had written a message:

Hey Mum and Dad,

Today was a disaster to begin with cos one of the calves escaped into a neighbour's garden and destroyed his flowers. HE WAS FUMING!!! I thought Uncle Henry would be furious cos there are some big money worries here right now, and he's not been himself lately. But, surprisingly, he thought it was funny. The neighbour wants Uncle Henry to pay for the damage and Nora told me they haven't got any insurance. I don't know what they're going to do about it. xx

Charity set her phone down, but it buzzed only seconds later. She was surprised to see a message from her mum had appeared almost instantly.

Hi Charity,

Oh no! That's awful! We'd heard they were in financial difficulty at the moment but didn't realise it was so bad. I hope you're well. Only business meetings at our end as usual, but you have just reminded me to call one of our old business partners up tomorrow. Keep me updated.

Charity grinned; her mum had responded! Within a few seconds, at that! She re-read the message again, before sending off a quick good-night message that was again responded to within minutes. Relaxing into her pillow, Charity settled down for a welcome sleep. One thing wouldn't stop nagging at her though. How did her parents know about the farm's financial difficulties? They were always too busy to stay in touch with their relatives so she doubted that her aunt or uncle would have told them. And how had Charity's text reminded her mum about an old business friend? She frowned as she went over things in her head.

After puzzling over these questions for a few minutes, she decided that it wasn't entirely impossible that her aunt or uncle would have mentioned it to her dad when they arranged for Charity to stay over for the summer.

A warm wet lick disturbed her train of thought and she turned to see the farm's sheepdog, Skye, gazing playfully into her eyes.

"Oh, not you as well." She was reminded of that morning when she was awoken by Gwen the goat in her room. "Go away," Charity groaned. Skye whined for several minutes.

"Skye!" she cried, "Oh come on then," Charity said, patting the space next to her for Skye to lie beside her. The collie jumped up and made herself comfortable whilst Charity stroked her. "I bet Nora's got you doing this. Uncle Henry would go mad if he knew she's got half the farmyard coming up to the bedrooms. Tomorrow it'll probably be a goose on the bed!"

Just as she was falling asleep, Charity heard her door burst open and Nora rushed in.

"What the?" groaned Charity.

"Shhhh, Mum and Dad are having a conversation about old Reek, come on!" Nora signalled for Charity to follow. The girls crept out onto the landing, Skye's nails clicking on the floorboards, then down the staircase, before stopping at the bend so they could listen without being seen. They could hear Uncle Henry and Aunt Sarah having a heated discussion in the kitchen.

"I can't believe he would ask us for that kind of money when he knows we don't have it!' Uncle Henry said disdainfully.

"I know, but we can't exactly refuse to pay for what Milo wrecked," Aunt Sarah replied.

"Well what will we pay him with, cows? Milo only ate his flowers! It wouldn't cost anywhere near what he's asking for to repair the damage. He's only doing this because he didn't get his own way about our business."

"Dad and Reek were business partners?" Nora hissed to Charity.

Charity pulled a confused face.

"But that was years ago." They heard Alfie's voice join the conversation. Nora's eyes widened in disbelief when she heard her brother's voice.

"And Alfie knows?" Nora hissed indignantly." That's SO not fair!"

"Well, people can hold grudges for a long time," Sarah offered.

"Yes, well, it's not my fault our plans for the business didn't work out."

"It wasn't only old Reeker. Uncle Richard had his plans spoiled too," pointed out Alfie.

Charity's ears pricked up at the mention of her father. Both girls frowned at each other, trying to work out what was going on here. Mr

Reekworth and Charity's father knew each other? What was this talk about plans and business that seemed to connect the three men?

"Yes, but my brother doesn't constantly complain and make things difficult for me out of spite for it! He's got on with his life and built a business himself. In fact, so has Reeky; driving around in that silly banana-mobile. He's obviously done alright for himself. I'm the one who's suffered here, not them."

Alfie yawned. "I'm heading up to bed. I've got milking at 4 am."

Nora and Charity jumped up and ran back up the stairs as they heard the sound of shifting chairs from below. Charity, leaping onto her bed, heard the sound of a slamming door and Nora throwing something at the wall separating the two rooms. She could tell that her cousin felt hurt, having been left out of a family secret. Charity got back into bed, but lay wide awake, her thoughts thundering through her mind. The last thing that went through her head before she finally fell into a restless sleep was, *What's my dad got to do with this?*

CHAPTER 6

A PIECE OF THE PUZZLE

Charity's father was filling Gwen the goat in all about the farm's financial problems. Gwen looked up from the book she was reading as she suggested the best ways to fix them. Charity's father was interrupted as Rowan rode regally into the room on the back of a goose and asked if anyone wanted a cup of tea. Suddenly the goose took flight, toppling Rowan head-first into a goldfish bowl where he turned into a crab. "Charity! Get up, now!" The goose honked at her.

Charity sat bolt upright in bed, her eyes staring. She blinked and it took a few seconds before she realised she was still in the spare bedroom on her uncle's farm, and it had just been a strange dream.

Her inky hair was a mass of frizz and engulfed her face. She quickly grabbed her phone from the bedside table, trying to rid herself of the image of Rowan riding a goose, that seemed imprinted on her memory. A quick glance at the screen showed her there were no messages or notifications.

She slumped out of bed and shuffled towards the door, trying to smooth her static hair into a bobble. Pulling open the door and starting towards the staircase, her mind was consumed by what she'd heard last night and the weird dream she'd just had.

HOOONNNNNKKKKKKK!

Charity blinked and stopped. Was she still dreaming? There was a goose right outside her room.

THUD!

A white egg landed on the carpet in the doorway. The goose began to preen its feathers as if nothing had happened.

"THERE'S A GOOSE ON THE LANDING," she screamed. The startled goose flapped its gigantic ivory wings and hissed before it waddled towards the top of the stairs where it paused.

"AND ITS LAID AN EGG!"

The ungainly hobbled clumsily down the creaky stairs with Charity rushing after it into the kitchen. "Come here, you ruddy goose!" She chased it around the table legs for a minute, trying and failing to herd it towards the door that she'd opened into the farmyard. Rather than heading out of the house, the goose turned on Charity. It lowered its long white neck and hissed, before snaking towards her and grabbing the hem of her pyjama bottoms. It tugged so hard Charity almost lost her balance. She screamed and the goose released her momentarily but then it came at her again, ready for a second grab. Charity recoiled when she saw the inside of the goose's open beak – it seemed to have teeth *on its tongue*! She leapt onto a chair to take refuge on the kitchen table. The goose tilted its head and viewed her with a beady blue eye as she screamed, "Help!"

Rowan pirouetted into the room, still in his pyjamas. Charity blinked in disbelief again as she took in his bright pink lobster onesie.

"I will save you, sweet damsel in distress!" he declared, bowing low, one of his 'claws' sweeping the floor.

"Oh, thanks, Rowan."

"I was talking to Guieseppe the Second, not *you*."

"What? Who's Guiesesppe?"

"The goose, duh!"

Charity's fists closed and she rested them on her hips as she stared at the lobster, now on his knees, crawling under the table like a true bottom feeder

"Okay, A, why does a female goose have a boy's name, and B, why is she Guieseppe *the Second*?"

Rowan's voice was muffled and she had to bend over to hear him.

"We didn't know he was a she until he she laid an egg. Plus, female geese aren't usually aggressive, so we assumed she was a gander.

She tries to attack everyone except me for some reason. She's a great guard goose, miles scarier than the dog. And there's a sad story about Guieseppe the First involving a tractor. Tragic." He started to hum the tune to the song, *Tragedy*.

Charity straightened up, shaking her head incredulously. Her dream had been strange but reality was even stranger. As she stepped down from the table onto a chair, Rowan came reversing out from under the table, Guieseppe the Second clutched between his claws.

"I have saved you, my lady!" Rowan planted a kiss on top of the goose's head and then moonwalked from the room, taking the goose with him.

After breakfast, Aunt Sarah took Rowan off to his Young Actors holiday club. He was delighted as it meant he got out of helping Alfie and the girls to muck out the calf stable. Uncle Henry had eaten a quick (goose) egg sandwich, gulped down a mug of tea after the milking and rushed off to an auction to try and get some spare parts for the JCB loadall, since they couldn't do without it on the farm and the tines on the fork had suddenly snapped yesterday. Henry couldn't understand what had happened: they weren't rusty or old. There was no reason he could think of to explain them breaking. But the loadall was the most important machine on the farm so it had to be fixed. With him and Sarah gone, that meant Alfie was left in charge.

"Come on then, you two. The sooner we get started, the sooner we finish. It shouldn't take too long with three of us doing it."

The three of them, accompanied by Skye the dog, headed towards the calves' stable to begin clearing out the dirty straw. On their way, they stopped at the outbuilding where the yard tools were kept to pick up the equipment they needed. As they neared it, Alfie took a key from his overall pocket to unlock the padlock on the door.

"Hang on a minute," he said, noticing that the door was not only unlocked, but slightly ajar. "Why isn't this locked?"

"Maybe Dad needed to get something out of there before he rushed off. He could've forgotten to lock it again."

"Yeah, probably. He knew we'd be coming in here to get stuff so he must've just left it open for us." Alfie shrugged and pushed the door open.

"HOLY COW!" he gasped.

"What?!" cried Nora. "What is it, Alfie? Let me see!" She elbowed him out of the way. As Nora pushed her way into the shed, Charity caught a glimpse of the interior. Now she could see what had shocked Alfie… Inside was complete carnage; rakes, shovels, axes, spades and pitchforks were all over the floor and some had even been snapped in the middle. The wheelbarrow was tipped on its side with massive slashes in its tyre and one of the handles had been fractured. The toolbox had been smashed on the floor in a crazy heap of spanners and screwdrivers. Charity knew very little about tool sheds but even she knew that they weren't supposed to look like this. This was, well… a bomb site! Standing in the middle of the chaos, innocently chewing on a gardening glove, was Gwen.

"What's happened here?" Nora gasped in horror, breaking the astounded silence.

"And what are we going to do?" Charity muttered.

"I'm going to call Dad, you can take some pictures of this to show him, then we'd better try and tidy it up." Alfie commanded, reaching into his pocket for his phone, muttering under his breath, "Dad'll have a heart attack if he sees it like this."

For the next three hours, the trio worked non-stop to clean up the mess. Uncle Henry had abandoned the auction as soon as he received the call from Alfie and had arrived halfway through the clean up to see the mess for himself.

"Why would anyone do something like this?" Nora asked her father once he had recovered from the shock of seeing his precious tools in ruins.

"I don't know love."

"Do you think it was Mr Reekworth?" Charity suggested.

"No," he said "I know he doesn't like us but he wouldn't stoop so low. For one, he wouldn't know how important our tool shed is, let alone where to find it."

Even though Charity believed Uncle Henry, she still felt that Mr Reekworth had something to do with the incident. She remembered how furious he was when Milo destroyed his garden and the murderous look in his eyes as he'd shouted at them. If a person looked like they were about to strangle someone when their flowers had been eaten, Charity wouldn't put it past them to commit a crime like this one.

Once the shed had been tidied, the group retired to the farmhouse kitchen, where they sat in stony silence, drinking tea or hot chocolate, each person immersed in their own thoughts and questions.

Aunt Sarah returned mid-afternoon with shopping bags in hand and a concerned expression on her face. As she dumped the bags wearily on the floor, Rowan whizzed into the room on his knees. "Never fear loyal subjects. I have returned!" he cried wielding a plastic spatula he'd seized from the worktop as he sailed past.

"Let's see it then," sighed Aunt Sarah, ignoring her son

Charity and Nora volunteered to show her all the broken tools that they had tidied into a pile with what was left from the shed. After Aunt Sarah had seen it all, she turned silently and went back to the farmhouse.

Just as Charity was about to shut the door to the shed and follow her aunt, she noticed something glinting in the afternoon light. She approached the back corner and picked up the mystery object.

"Nora!" she exclaimed, holding up what appeared to be an expensive ring. Its huge diamond reflected prisms of coloured light like a miniature disco ball.

"Woah!" said Nora. "That's fancy!"

"Is it your mum's?"

"I don't recognise it. She doesn't really wear rings anymore but it might be. She used to wear rings when she worked as a project manager."

"When did she do that?"

"She used to work for this big business and was high up in the company before she married Dad and moved onto the farm. She earned loads from it apparently."

"Why did she stop then?" Charity asked.

"Oh, you know, she was looking after us and Dad needed help here so she gave it up."

"Oh." Charity pocketed the ring for safekeeping, meaning to ask Aunt Sarah about it later

The two girls left the shed and headed back to the farmhouse. On the way, Charity's mind was working in a frenzy. Her thoughts rushed around her head as they walked. The finding of the ring had triggered a sliver of memory that she couldn't quite bring to mind. She wondered why Aunt Sarah's ring had been amongst all the damage. One part of her was telling herself that her aunt had simply been wearing it when she had last gone into the shed and it had slipped off, but another deeper, darker part of her suspected that she may have had something to do with the vandalism. *But Aunt Sarah would never do something like that to her own farm. Would she?*

The rest of the day was spent in bitter silence as everyone got on with their jobs. When darkness fell, they all finally retired to bed after a slightly sad dinner of soup. Charity sat cross-legged on her bed, stroking Skye who'd followed her up the stairs and into her room, feeling slightly sorry for herself. She felt a sudden wave of homesickness which she couldn't explain since she'd never really liked being at home anyway. But she couldn't deny that she was feeling slightly lonely since no-one had spoken much after the morning's incident. She took her phone out of her bag and started to text her mother:

Hi, how's things with u + Dad? We had a bad day here today somebody broke into the tool shed and smashed up everything in it!!!!! Shocking!

An unusually quick reply pinged just as she was about to put her phone down.

Oh no, that is bad luck. Poor Henry and Sarah. That's the last thing they need. We're fine but really busy as usual. It'll just be young vandals in the shed, I'm sure there'll be no more trouble xx

Charity typed out,

Not sure about that. I found a ring in all the mess. Wondered if it might be Aunt Sarah's?? She can't have had anything to do with it???!! I hope the farm will return to normal soon since it could be so much fun. It's bonkers here!!!

A few moments later, another reply appeared.

The ring will be Sarah's. Who else's would it be? Sarah wouldn't have vandalised her own property, she just probably dropped it one time. I hope they catch whoever did it, the bunch of hooligans. See u soon xx

Maybe, but I feel like I've seen the ring before…? Charity messaged back.

Charity had forgotten to show the ring to Aunt Sarah. It was still in her pocket. She fished it out and snapped a picture of it, then sent it on to her mother. She watched the dots that appeared to indicate her mother was typing something back, but it took several minutes before the reply finally appeared.

I wouldn't give the ring back to Sarah. Don't show it to anyone. Better just keep it somewhere safe for now.

Her mother was probably right: Aunt Sarah must've dropped the ring sometime in the past and not known where she'd lost it. But Charity was puzzled that her mum didn't want her to give the ring back. Why not? She held it up to her face and inspected it closely. The ring shimmered as she examined it, as if it was winking at her. Again, the vague memory that seemed to go with the ring popped back into her head but she couldn't figure it out. She felt like she had seen it before but she didn't know where. Maybe Aunt Sarah had been wearing it when Charity had visited the farm in the past.

Yes, that was it! She couldn't have seen it anywhere else.

Charity put her phone on the bedside table and put the ring in her sock drawer so she could get changed for bed. That night she fell into a deep sleep, but now and then the ring popped in and out of her dreams as if it wanted her to remember something.

CHAPTER 7

WHO LET THE COWS OUT?

A week had passed but Charity still tossed and turned in her sleep, trying to make sense of everything that had occurred. Three more incidents had taken place since the tool shed was vandalised: the chicken shed had been opened one night and a fox got in with the inevitable result (Rowan *swore* he had locked them in), the bags of milk formula for the calves had been ripped open and spoiled and, to top it all, the farmyard had been flooded when a tap was left running all night. That had caused a hectic morning of rescuing tools, food and animals from the waterlogged outbuildings. Everyone was suspicious about whether these were coincidences or if someone was behind it, but each time no clues were left: not even a single footprint, so no-one knew for sure.

Uncle Henry and Aunt Sarah looked even more worn out than when Charity had arrived. It was definitely not turning into the fun-filled summer at the farm Charity had hoped for. She thought that her presence was probably one more thing for them to worry about, and wondered if she should go home. But at least she could be of help here, whilst home was brutally boring. *But* she thought, selfishly, *I'm spending all my holidays doing hard, dirty work.*

This is so unfair. She pictured her friend, Sophie, enjoying the white beaches of Thailand and her sister on her US adventure, and sighed deeply. Why couldn't that be her?

***

Charity woke to the second week of the summer holidays, from a series of short, strange dreams filled with the ring, trying to chase it as it rolled down a steep, grassy hill. She tripped over a grassy tussock and fell head-first, about to hit the coarse ground when she stirred from her tormenting dream. Opening the drawer of her bedside table, and searching among her socks, she scowled as the ring glinted at her innocently from its hiding place.

As Charity walked along the landing, stretching her stiff limbs, she was swallowed up by an intense silence. All the doors were open apart from Nora's. It looked like the two girls had been left behind. Charity took it that Nora was still asleep, but it was hard to know as her door was *always* closed... though was it open a crack? Charity swung around, waiting for her cousin. But no-one appeared. "Nora?" She called, knocking on the door. There was no reply, but she could hear some scuffling sounds from within. Glancing around, she pressed the handle and slipped through the door, keen to get a look at what lay beyond the 'KEEP OUT OR YOU DIE!' sign hung on the door.

Charity was surprised to see that her cousin wasn't in the room. But although she found it unoccupied, it was far from being empty: it was an explosion of animals! There were several rabbits in homemade hutches, a magpie perched on the curtain rail – which was clearly its favourite spot judging by the trail of bird poo that striped the purple curtains. A hedgehog was curled up in a hamster cage on Nora's desk, while a toad sat beside it, rather filling the goldfish bowl it was kept in. *This is chaos,* thought Charity, imagining what her mother would think as she carefully picked her way through the animal care manuals that littered the floor. She scrambled her way towards the window overlooking the yard and crinkled her nose at the less-than-fresh smell in the room. Charity reached for the window latch and almost opened it before she remembered the magpie. "Better not let you out." She looked up at the bird who had an imperious eye fixed on her. "Nora would never forgive me!"

Charity heaved another sigh. I knew Nora liked animals, but I didn't know that she kept a hoard of them in her bedroom. Then it dawned on her on why she wouldn't let anyone into her room. She doesn't want her parents to know she has a zoo in here! Charity stared around the room, taking in Nora's secret.

Many posters of animals and reminders of the local animal shelter's annual adoption fairs were stuck all over the princess wallpaper; pink tiaras peeked through here and there. Obviously, Nora was well out of her princess phase. Charity backed out and shut the door. Still walking backwards towards the landing, she tripped over a mislaid shoe and fell flat on her bum. Grumbling, she got back to her feet, wondering where everyone was, and feeling rather sulky that they'd all gone and left her.

Charity wandered into the empty kitchen.

"Hello?" she called, but there was no reply. Her skin prickled with the silence of the house. It was never silent. Charity would even have been happy to see Rowan in his pink lobster onesie. Collapsing onto a kitchen chair, she wondered what to do. A cold breeze made her shudder and she realised that the front door was ajar. "What is it with this house and its self-opening doors? Is there a gremlin or a ghoul living here?" she muttered to herself. Suddenly, a black shadow stretched towards her like a giant dark tongue. Her eyes grew wide but then the shadow shrunk and shrivelled to a much smaller size as Guieseppe walked into the kitchen, flexing her wings.

"Oh no you don't. Not again!" huffed Charity, swiftly grabbing a broom and brandishing it at Guiseppe like a weapon. "OUT," she yelled, chasing the goose back out into the yard. Guiseppe honked and hissed, scandalised.

Charity stood in the doorway, watching the goose strut away. An image of Rowan popped into her head. *Wow, Rowan walks just like that goose!* It occurred to her.

Well, if no-one is going to come looking for me, I'll go looking for them.

She shoved on some wellies and a jacket and headed out of the door, hoping to find her uncle, aunt and cousins. The morning was dull and grey again with a most un-summerly cold wind snaking around the yard. She zipped up her jacket to block out the chill that stabbed through her thin T-shirt. She checked everywhere – all the barns and outbuildings – but there was no-one to be seen. It took her a moment to notice what else seemed wrong… it was a dairy farm… with no cows! There wasn't a sight nor sound of a single cow or calf. If it hadn't been for the sight of Guieseppe and Nora's zoo, Charity might have believed the place was deserted.

Pushing down the panic uncoiling inside her, she tried to think what to do. The cows had all gone and the family had disappeared too. What could have happened? A sudden noise from the farmhouse made her jump. It was the sound of a phone ringing. The house phone.

Stumbling, Charity rushed back to the farmhouse and flung off her wellies at the door. She looked around, wondering where the phone was. She'd never used it before. By the time she'd located it in the hallway, the phone stopped ringing just as she grabbed it. "Holy cow!" she exclaimed, picking up Alfie's phrase. She stared at it, willing it to ring again, but it just sat there and stared back at her in stubborn silence. Giving up, she ran to her room, in search of her mobile. The mutinous house phone had given her an idea.

Typing in Nora's number, she had barely pressed the speaker button before her cousin's voice blasted out at her.

"Charity! Oh, thank god you've answered. I tried ringing you then I tried the house phone."

"I left my phone in my room. I was outside looking for you and didn't make it back in time to answer your call. Where are you all? Do you know there's no sign of any of the cows?"

"Of course! That's where we are! We've been in the village since dawn, trying to round them all up. Someone let them out in the night. Dad and Alfie discovered that they were all missing when they went out to milk this morning. They made such a racket waking Mum up that Rowan and I got up and went to help. Those pesky cows are all over the village! They've destroyed it! They've trampled gardens, dented cars, knocked wing mirrors off, they've pooed *everywhere* – it's such a mess. The villagers have called the police and they're here helping to round them up. Some of Dad's farmer friends have come to help too. It was all too much for poor Skye. She's absolutely shattered!"

As Nora paused for breath, Charity caught a glimpse of a blue flashing light from outside her bedroom window.

"Why didn't you wake me up as well?" she asked. "I could've come to help."

"I can't believe you slept through us all banging about. You must sleep like a log! I asked Mum about waking you but she said to let you sleep. Said our problems aren't your problems and you shouldn't have to get involved."

"Still, you could have left a note or something." Charity grumbled, but Nora didn't hear as she was already halfway across the field.

***

After the cows had been rounded up and returned to Hazel Tree Farm, the family gave a collective sigh as they realised that they had to go and face the angry villagers and the formidable Parish Council to help clear up the mess.

"It's about time you got here! We've been waiting for over an hour!" Mr Reekworth spat with disdain.

"We haven't been an *hour* and..." Alfie broke off after a glare from his mum.

"Don't you test me boy!" Mr Reekworth said.

"Anyway, shall we get on with the cleaning?" Nora asked, seeing Alfie about to retort and pinching his arm aggressively.

"Oww! What was that for?" Alfie glared at his sister.

The next few hours were spent cleaning away the worst of the mess from the village. The damaged items would need to be dealt with another day. By the time they had finished everyone was tired beyond belief and looking forward to going back to the house for a nice warm cuppa.

When Charity entered her room to change her filthy clothes, she knew immediately that something was wrong. Although her laptop was still open where she'd left it and her bed was still unmade, some of the items of clothing she'd left dumped on the floor in untidy piles had been folded and stacked neatly. They were still on the floor but Charity knew for a fact that she hadn't folded them up. She didn't *do* folding. She was about to shout down the stairs to ask if anyone had been in her room but she changed her mind. She knew no-one had as they'd all been out dealing with the escaped cows all day. And if Aunt Sarah had been in to tidy up, there was no way she'd have gone to the trouble of folding Charity's clothes just to leave them on the floor. She'd have hung them up, put them in drawers, or at the very least, placed them on the bed for Charity to put away. She turned slowly around, noticing as much as she could. Her pens and paper were still strewn over her desk, her headphones still dangled from the lampshade on the bedside table and a plate full of crumbs from a biscuit snack she'd had still sat on the floor beside the bed where she'd left it.

Charity couldn't shake the sense that someone had been in her room. Unless there was a ghost or house-elf with a penchant for folding clothes, someone had done that. But why? And if they were so concerned with her room being tidy, there was plenty of other mess they could have dealt with. Her eyes suddenly swept to the bedside table again. Darting towards it, she wrenched open the top drawer and scanned the contents. All her socks were still in the messy muddle they'd been in that morning. She found the ones decorated with tiny pandas and felt for the hardness of the ring hidden inside one of them. Nothing but soft fluffiness greeted her fingers. She pulled them apart and burrowed deep into both socks individually, but there was nothing there.

CHAPTER 8

THE PUZZLE IS SOLVED?

The ring was gone. It wasn't in the sock drawer. It wasn't on top of the dressing table beside the lamp and it wasn't even on the floor or under the bed where it could have fallen. Putting her hands on her hips, Charity looked around the room again, frowning.

“Charity!” Nora’s voice cut through her thoughts.

Charity reluctantly gave up her search and made her way to Nora’s bedroom. Knowing what was inside, she pushed the door open a crack and peered in, taking care not to let anything fly, hop or scuttle out past her.

“Shhh,” Nora whispered, grabbing Charity’s arm and tugging her into the room “Quickly.”

“Whoa! What is it?” Charity asked, swerving around the animal littered floor.

“Mind the duck. And you’re sworn to secrecy about what you see in here, by the way. No-one else knows.” Charity nodded, not wanting to let on that she already knew about Nora’s secret zoo. “You’ll never believe what I found out.” She pushed Charity down onto her bed, while she paced in front of her. “You know how Grandad was the original owner of the farm? Well, our dads helped him with it when they were younger but neither of them wanted to farm forever and they made plans to turn it into an electronics business that they would run together when Grandad retired. But Grandad didn't like the sound of that, so he insisted that it stayed a working farm and placed a covenant on it so that it couldn't be used for anything else. After much persuasion, from Grandad, my dad took it on. Your dad and his business partner at the time "old Reeky", were really mad since they'd already spent money on the electronics company and so our dads fell out big time."

"Hold on… My dad was in business with Mr Reekworth?!" Charity exclaimed, a look of disbelief on her face. Nora continued her story, taking care not to step on the duck and its brood of fluffy yellow ducklings which had emerged from under the bed, cheeping merrily.

"Apparently our dads ignored each other for *years* and didn't even attend each other's weddings! It was only when Alfie was born that they decided to try and make up. But they're still a bit cold towards each other even today, as we both know."

"What? How come I've never heard anything about this?" Charity asked. But then she remembered that her parents never told her anything anyway, never mind things about their past. "Actually, don't answer that. How do you know all this?"

"Last night, Mum asked me to help her sort through some old documents to see if had any insurance papers for the damage to the village and I spotted this cardboard folder full of old letters

Anyway, I sneaked it out, and last night, in bed, I read through them and worked it all out.."

As Nora spoke, something clicked in Charity's mind. "Oh, hold on … so what if the vandal is Mr Reekworth getting revenge on your dad for taking on the farm and ruining his and my dad's plans?"

"That's what I was thinking!" Nora exclaimed. "As I read the letters, I thought about how much old Reeky hates us and how the vandal must be someone who lives close to us and he ticks all the boxes."

"You're right," Charity said. She beamed and Nora grinned back. "Have we just figured out who's been attacking the farm?"

But before Nora could say anything more, Rowan came bursting in.

"Drumroll, please. Here is the magnificent, marvellous and magical Rowan at your service! A drink of the elixir of life ladies?" He presented a goblet containing some unrecognisable liquid.

"I think I'll pass."

"Err, no thanks," Charity and Nora answered in unison.

"Okay my princesses, other citizens await my assistance. Come forth my knights, we shall battle on!" He finished his sentence, talking to the empty space in front of him, before striding out again.

"Well that was interesting, I wonder if that's part of Rowan's play he's practising for?" Charity asked.

"Not likely, he's doing Beauty and the Lobster as his final performance," Nora replied.

"That explains the lobster onesie then."

"Charity, Nora, Rowan, where are you? PC Holmes is here." Aunt Sarah shouted up the stairs. The three of them bounded down, with Rowan making sure he was the first to the bottom.

"Rowan the magnificent…"

"No time for acting Rowan, this is serious," Aunt Sarah insisted.

They entered the kitchen where Henry was sitting opposite a uniformed policewoman. Sarah sat beside him and the children hovered in the doorway.

"I want you to tell me anything you know about the recent incidents concerning the farm. Can you show me where the events took place so I can collect some evidence?" PC Holmes said.

"I'm sorry officer, we don't have any evidence to show you." Aunt Sarah looked concerned.

Charity felt a hot blush rising up her neck and her eyes darted to the floor. "Err, we did have a ring..." she muttered. "We found it in the tool shed after it had been vandalised."

"A ring you say? Do you have it?" The officer pounced on the information like a panther, while Aunt Sarah's face was a map of confusion and concern.

"I…I can't find it. I think it's been taken, as it isn't where I hid it. I've looked all over for it." Charity felt herself shrinking under her aunt and uncle's gaze. There were looking at her like she was a thief.

"I'm afraid I can't help you if you don't have any evidence. We can do a check for fingerprints but it's not likely to help us catch them. If you do find anything, be sure to contact us." PC Holmes strode to the door and left.

"Yes of course." Aunt Sarah said with a slightly sad tone to her voice.

If only I had that ring, Charity thought to herself. But Norah's voice brought her back to reality.

"Mum, Dad! Charity and I think we know who the culprit is."

"What?" Uncle Henry asked wearily.

"Who?" Aunt Sarah inquired.

"Well… Charity and I think it's Mr Reekworth." Nora said grinning proudly.

Uncle Henry's posture seemed to sag even more. "Oh, girls, I don't think–"

"No, no, hear me out!" Nora said, cutting him off. Mr Reekworth hates our family because you ruined his plans by taking on the farm all those years ago and–"

"How do you know about that?" Uncle Henry asked, his eyes wide with shock.

Nora swatted the question away like a fly with her hand. "So, Mr Reekworth hates us and he lives close enough to get away to safety quickly after attacking and he also has good contacts with people like the police and so could get out of trouble easily. He's just the perfect fit for causing all the trouble."

Uncle Henry sighed. "Look, girls. I appreciate your concern about the farm and I understand that Mr Reekworth strongly dislikes us but I don't think he would stoop that low."

"But why not?" Nora whined.

"Nora, honey, Mr Reekworth may be a bit unpleasant but he's not behind all of this. If he'd wanted some sort of revenge, I don't think he'd have waited all these years. And anyway, it was your grandad's fault for putting the covenant on the farm, not mine. Now, why don't you all forget about it and try to enjoy your summer holiday?"

Charity and Rowan walked solemnly back upstairs and Nora followed, taking all of her washing with her so that her mother had no reason to enter her room. They left the adults deep in conversation at the kitchen table.

***

At dinner that night everybody seemed quiet – even Rowan didn't make one of his 'amazing' entrances. Finally breaking the silence, Uncle Henry turned to Alfie.

"Tomorrow we'll go and get that quad bike I saw advertised in The Gazette. The old one would cost too much to repair and we can't manage without one."

"Oh. Right," Alfie said, dropping some peas off his fork. "But… err… I thought we couldn't afford a new one?"

"Well, it's second hand and I…I've managed to get hold of some money, so…" he trailed off, staring down at his plate.

"But what if something happens to it? I've got a feeling that whoever is doing all these things will see something new and want to wreck it." Alfie leant back in his chair and folded his arms across his chest. "I don't know if it's a good idea to spend money on something that might just get vandalised. Since the police can't help and we can't afford to set up CCTV, how safe will it be?"

Henry and Sarah looked at each other and acknowledged Alfie's concern. "Well, while there's hardly any silage in the silage barn, we'll keep it locked up in there with the tractors. And… we have a plan." Sarah said, taking a deep breath. "The three of us are going to do shifts of staying up through the night and popping out to check the yard. Hopefully, if anyone is loitering around looking to cause trouble, they'll see us going out, and be put off. They won't want to risk being caught." Her voice was bright as she said this, but the bags under her eyes disagreed with her words.

"Oh, we can help!" Piped Rowan, gesturing at himself and the girls. "It'd be like being a spy.

I can be Double-O-Rowan. I'll have night vision goggles and–"

"No Rowan. You'll be going to bed, I'm afraid, as will the girls. This is an adults-only mission," his mother said. "You just concentrate on learning your lines for the play. It's not far away now."

Rowan immediately went into character and said sincerely, *"Think of the one thing that you've always wanted. Now find it in your mind's eye and feel it in your heart."* He reached into the air with his left hand before pulling it back towards his chest and clutching his hands over his heart.

Immediately distracted, Rowan slid from his chair and floated around the house where he could be heard delivering his lines with gusto from every room for the rest of the evening.

Once everyone had helped tidy up after the meal, Henry went for a nap as he would be taking the first shift that night. Everyone else collapsed on the sofa to watch some TV before bed. Nora found an animal-based comedy on channel 33 and everyone was soon laughing along. It was just what they all needed to lighten the mood. Charity, however, was lost in her thoughts. If her aunt and uncle were certain Mr Reekworth had nothing to do with recent events, then who was behind it…and why?

Absently, Charity fired off a text to her mum to inform her of the day's disaster. She replied straight away. Several messages went back and forth as she relayed information about the police's visit and her suspicions about Mr Reekworth. Charity's mum gave her commiserations about the police's lack of ability to help and asked several questions about the new quad bike Charity had told her about. She, like Alfie, seemed concerned for its safety, but Charity reassured her by passing on the plans to keep it safe. Eventually, the messages stopped so Charity started to scroll through the pictures she had saved on her phone, deleting some of the ones that were accidental shots of the sky or the ground.

In no time, she'd gone back into pictures taken two years ago. She was just about to swipe past one, but then something caught her eye and she paused, bringing the phone closer to her face. Not convinced by what she was seeing, she zoomed in on a part of the picture. *No way,* she breathed. It couldn't be. She looked again. It was. Pieces clicked together in her mind like parts of a jigsaw puzzle, suddenly forming a full, clear picture.

Jolting upright, she scrambled around on the sofa for the TV remote and muted the movie. "Hey! What are you doing?" Nora yelled. "Put it back on!"

Alfie, who'd also been engrossed in his phone raised an eyebrow and looked questioningly at Charity. Fortunately, Aunt Sarah had fallen asleep, her empty mug dangling from her hand.

"I need to tell you guys something." Nora began to protest but Charity spoke over her. "No, it's urgent. I know who's behind all that's been going on here and I think I know how to catch them. But we need to work together. Listen up."

CHAPTER 9

SHOW TIME

After the constant rain at the beginning of the holidays, the sun seemed to remember that it was summer, and at last, it came out in force as Charity, Nora and Alfie scoped out the area for their plan. The farm seemed quiet as nothing had happened recently. The all-night surveillance appeared to be working as there had been no more mysterious disasters, but Charity was sure that tonight was the night that all hell would break loose. They had just finished a quick meeting about their plan for the evening.

Uncle Henry called to them as they walked, whispering to each other, back to the house, exclaiming, "Have you seen how much the grass has come up over these past few days?" He plucked a few strands from the garden to show them the improvement. "Soon we'll be able to cut the fields and have enough silage for the cows during winter!" Uncle Henry seemed to be in the highest spirits Charity had seen him in for a long time. Cheerily, he passed them as he headed to the barn where they had just been gathered. Now that they had finished planning the night ahead, they had no worries except for the next feed for the calves.

Rowan, on the other hand, had more things on this plate than the others. Or so he thought. His youth club performance, 'Beauty and the Lobster', was starting that night and Rowan was busy being dramatic in his onesie, practising his lines for the leading part. At the last minute, it seemed he wasn't keen on playing the part with his own Cumbrian accent and was trying out different accents. One minute he was a Scottish lobster, the next Welsh. But at least it kept him too busy to notice what the others were up to.

At breakfast, Nora took on the job of making sure her mum and dad went to Rowan's performance that night.

"Hey, Dad, you know Rowan's play starts this evening, don't you? You and Mum are going to watch?"

"Well, we thought maybe not on the first night. Let him have a couple of runs through without us there, and then we could all go and see it together on the last night."

"Oh no. Rowan should have support on his opening night! And you guys have been so stressed out recently, it would be nice for you two to have a break." Alfie insisted, a little too keenly.

Uncle Henry gave him a funny look. "Well, I suppose we could. But what about the farm? If we're all at the play, there'll be no-one here to keep an eye out for any trouble."

"I'll stay here and patrol. You won't be late back so it'll be fine."

"Are you sure? If you say so then." Aunt Sarah smiled hesitantly.

Alfie fist-bumped the air, which wasn't the best idea as this made Rowan think that Alfie didn't want to see him in the play. "At least my sister and *cousin* are coming to watch me, if my *brother* isn't interested." He said in a mellifluous French accent.

Charity glared at Nora. Great, now they were going to have to come up with a reason why they couldn't go that night, since Rowan was expecting them to be there.

After breakfast, and once everyone had gone outside to get on with various jobs, Charity pulled her phone out of her pocket and began to text her mum;

Hey, things are getting better at the farm. No more break-ins have happened since the cow accident and the grass is beginning to grow. Things are finally looking up.

She began to walk up to her room to change her jeans for a pair of shorts and within moments she heard the *PING* of a reply from her mother.

That's so good to hear, how's Uncle Henry?

He's doing fine since everything has calmed down. It's Rowan's play tonight so that'll be nice.

No further replies appeared, so, wedging her phone into her shorts' back pocket, she went outside to help fix some broken guttering and paint the barn doors. It was a lovely day. They had the radio playing in the yard, everyone fell over Gwen the goat at least once and Guieseppe stole a sandwich, some roasted peppers and a pork pie when Nora and Rowan produced a picnic to have in the garden. It was nice to have a pleasant, relaxing day where the worst problem anyone had to deal with was paint and moss in their hair.

Later that evening, as Henry and Sarah got themselves ready to go and watch Rowan, Charity and Nora made a mess of lined paper, newspapers, textbooks, colouring pencils, Sellotape, scissors and whatever other paraphernalia they could find and settled themselves in it, ready to look busy. Alfie stood in the doorway and gave them a thumbs up when he heard his parents coming down the stairs.

"Oh, what're you doing girls? You're not ready to go!" Sarah looked at her watch and frowned. It was time to leave. Rowan bobbed beside her, bursting with excitement.

"Mum, I've got loads of geography homework to do over the holidays and Charity's helping me with it. We've just made a good start with it and it's a big project, and really important," Nora said sweetly. "We thought we'd crack on and get it finished, now we've started, and then we three," she pointed at Alfie and Charity, "could go and see Rowan's play another night."

Rowan was now leaping about wildly in the kitchen. "Think of the one thing you've always wanted, my dear Guieseppe! Now find it in your mind's eye and feel it in your heart!" he exclaimed, holding up the surprised goose before it flapped from his reach and ran out the door. "Picture that warm sun gleaming on your finely feathered back!" He continued his chaotic prancing as Uncle Henry and Aunt Sarah gathered their jackets. Although it had begun to get warmer, the nights still held a chill.

"Are you sure? Okay then. Alfie will be here and we won't be all night so I'm sure you'll be fine," Aunt Sarah told them as she went into the kitchen where Alfie was seated at the table, innocently reading Farming Weekly. "Watch them, Alfie. I don't want to come back to see the house in ruins!" she joked, more light-hearted than before.

Outside, Uncle Henry was waiting patiently for them, his breath visible in the air. Rowan began twirling outside towards him followed by a somewhat hesitant Aunt Sarah. Charity and Nora remained with their pile of 'homework' until they were sure that the adults and Rowan were out of sight.

Finally, after waiting for the car to pull out of the yard and drive out of sight, they headed outside. Charity quickly motioned with her hand for the rest of her associates to follow her out to the barn. They crept across the yard to the barn like thieves. The newly painted barn doors squeaked as Charity forced them open, having removed the padlock. Nora went to her hiding spot, from where she could record with her phone without being seen. Alfie immediately scaled the ladder up to the hayloft to where they had already moved hay bales closer to the edge. Charity hid behind a bush from where she could see the barn. She was the lookout and it was her job to lock the vandals in the barn if they appeared. The padlock sat at her feet, oiled and ready.

Sitting in the centre of the barn, where they had pushed it was their bait: the new quad bike Uncle Henry had just bought. It gleamed in the sparse light that fell through the roof, looking new and shiny. Now all they had to do was wait.

CHAPTER 10

A GOAT, A GOOSE AND A LOBSTER

They had grabbed three Bob the Builder walkie-talkies from Rowan's room before they went out to begin their mission.

"What is this garbage?" Alfie had demanded when Nora handed him the blue and yellow block.

Nora glared at him. "Garbage. Really? You used to love using them. I remember Mum telling me that you would take them everywh–"

Alfie silenced her with an iron glare but snatched the walkie-talkie nonetheless. Nora stuck her nose in the air, turned away and gave Charity hers.

They'd been in position, waiting for half an hour. Charity was beginning to grow bored and cold. Her little hiding spot behind the bush didn't provide much shelter from the chill in the air. She shifted in her place, trying to get a different position but ended up even more uncomfortable as she accidentally sat on a garden rake concealed within the grass. Charity wondered if anyone was going to turn up.

After waiting some more, her muscles were stiff from sitting in the same position for so long and, since she had forgotten to bring a water bottle, she was becoming thirsty. She decided to suggest to Nora and Alfie that they should rethink their decision. She tried to get through to them on her walkie-talkie but all she heard was static. It clearly didn't have much range. Sighing, she threw it into the grass and crept towards the barn doors. Just as she was about to prise them open to slip inside, she heard a muffled, "Bob the Builder, can he fix it? Bob the Builder. Yes, he can!" coming from the grass behind her. She shook her head and slipped noiselessly into the barn.

"Alfie, I'm boreeeeed." Nora moaned.

"Shh," he hissed at her.

Nora replied with a slightly louder "Shhhhhh."

"Sh."

"Shhh"

"Shhhh!"

Their shushing competition got louder and louder, each one wanting to have the last shush, until Charity shifted slightly, creaking one of the floorboards under her weight. Silence.

"It's just me," Charity hissed.

"Charity, I didn't hear you come in." Nora laughed nervously. Alfie whistled a quiet tune nonchalantly from the darkness.

"I was just thinking," Charity began. "Well, maybe we should rethink our approach. We could be out here for hours and no-one could show up."

"We should wait a little longer. I have a good feeling about this." Alfie said decisively, and so Charity turned, ready to head back to her position. But before she could open the door, she heard voices outside. She froze. Whoever was there seemed to be fumbling with the door. Charity just managed to scuttle and hide in a shadowy corner in the rear of the barn. She was sure she couldn't be seen but her heart was determined to betray her, thumping like a marching band.

Suddenly, the barn doors were thrust open and two hooded figures, a shade darker than black, slunk in. From her position, Charity could just make out that one was tall and broad, the other was small and scrawny. An eerie silence filled the air. Gradually, they both began to approach the quad bike.

"Are you sure about this?" The taller one said in a deep whisper.

"Oh, just shut up and get on with it," the other snarled.

As soon as the sentence was finished, the smaller figure started viciously attacking the quad bike with a mallet, and the burly one quickly followed their lead.

This was Alfie's cue to start pushing the bales. He tried to push them all but they seemed to be too heavy and only one fell over the platform. The heavy hay bale tumbled to the floor and narrowly missed the vandals. They yelled and looked up, just as Alfie managed to push several more down. A dozen bales of hay rained down on the pair, who screamed and shouted as they tried to dodge the falling bricks of hay and attempted to make for the door.

"Get the door Charity!" Alfie shouted.

Charity sprinted out from her hiding spot and ran as fast as she could towards the door. But before she could reach her target, she was struck by a falling bale. It was like being hit by a bomb falling out of the sky. Charity was bowled sideways and fell beside the smaller vandal, who was also hit. Stunned, Charity scrambled up again. She glanced at the smaller attacker sprawled on the floor by her feet. They were pinned underneath one of the bales which had landed right on top of them.

The other vandal was more agile and had managed to dodge all of the bales Alfie threw at him. He was sprinting and had nearly reached the door, not stopping to help his partner in crime.

"THE DOOR, CHARITY!" Alfie shouted urgently.

Still dazed, Charity picked herself up and made for the door. But as she sped forward, a sudden blow from the running figure sent her flying. She smacked onto to the cold, hard ground. From her sprawled position on the floor, Charity watched helplessly as the taller vandal disappeared out of the barn doors and into the night.

"Are you okay, Charity?" Nora asked, running over to help her up.

"Yes, I'm fine, but one of them got away."

"We'll catch them, don't worry. As long as you're ok that's all that matters."

"Did you get it all on your phone?" Charity panted, winded.

"Yep, all of it," Nora said proudly.

"Gotcha!" They heard Alfie's voice behind them. When they looked, they saw he had hold of the hay-bale-victim. They had been wriggling out from their confinement but Alfie had dropped out of the hayloft just in time to rugby tackle them and pin them back to the ground again.

A muffled scream escaped from the dark figure. Alfie stood up, hauling them to their feet. The mask had slipped, revealing part of their face.

"Just what we thought." Alfie threw the mask onto the floor, and moved aside so Charity and Nora could see who it was. The face of Charity's mum came into view.

"Charity! How could you do this to me?" Her mother's face was scrunched like a crumpled tissue as she spat the accusation at her daughter.

Anger surged through Charity's body. She had known this was going to happen, but coming face to face with the truth banished any hope that she might've been wrong. Hurt and confusion burned through her.

"*Why* Mum? Why would you do this?" Charity looked at the face she barely recognised, cradling her painful right arm to her chest. "To your own family?" Her voice trembled.

Before she had time to reply, the interrogation was interrupted by a noise from outside the barn. Gripping his aunt firmly by the wrists, Alfie steered her towards the barn door. Nora opened it wide enough for them all to fit through to see what was causing the commotion in the yard. "AAAARRRRGGGHHHHHH! Get OFF!" The other dark figure was on the ground, having tripped over Gwen the goat in his hurry to get away. Now he was being restrained by an irascible Giueseppe who had lunged at him and grabbed the bare skin on one of his wrists. She was locked on and refused to let go. The intruder writhed in agony. Charity winced.

The spectators watched from a safe distance, not sure what to do. None of them wanted to deal with the angry guard goose. Gwen the goat was not intimidated and was joining in with the fun by pulling on the already loose mask.

"Guieseppe!" They heard a voice float towards them. "Unhand that man this moment!" A lobster appeared through the gate and Guieseppe released her vicious grip, honking with joy as she ran, flapping her mighty wings, towards Rowan, still in his lobster costume.

Rowan seemed completely oblivious to the scenario in front of him. "I was fab-u-lous darlings!" he announced. "The star of the show!"

"What on earth is going on here?" Uncle Henry appeared behind him, his face like thunder as he saw his brother looking up at him from the ground.

"I…I can explain!" Charity's father grimaced, clutching his bleeding wrist. "I…"

"I'd *love* to hear it." There was no mistaking Henry's sarcasm as he watched his brother scramble to his feet. Henry didn't help him up.

"Where are the girls?" Aunt Sarah interrupted, before Charity's father could speak again. She could see Alfie, still holding onto Charity's mother who looked like she wanted to scratch someone's eyes out, but there was no sign of Nora and Charity.

Alfie looked around him. He hadn't noticed that they were gone.

Blue lights flashed into the yard as a police car pulled up and an officer climbed out. "We've had a report of a disturbance and vandalism on these premises," he began, taking in the curious scene before him which included a man on the ground, a goose, a goat and a lobster. He blinked a few times to make sure it was not a dream.

"Yes, that's right." Charity said, appearing with Nora from the house. "It was me who called you. These people are the ones responsible for all the awful things that have been happening here recently. We've got video evidence to prove it."

Nora approached the officer with her phone and played the video showing the pair smashing up the quad bike. The officer's face hardened as he watched the scene unfold.

"Charity! How *could* you?" her mother repeated, incredulously.

Charity threw a cold stare at her mother. "I could ask you the same thing." All eyes were on her and even Rowan couldn't think of anything to say as the realisation of what had just happened sunk in.

They all watched in disbelief as the pair were bundled into the police car and driven away.

CHAPTER 11

HOW TO EAT A KIT KAT

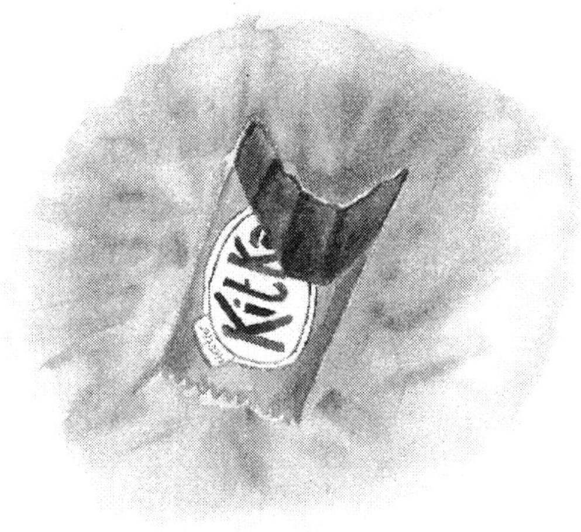

Poor Rowan's limelight was unceremoniously switched off. Instead of him glorying in re-living his debut on the stage for everyone's benefit, he was shushed loudly. Henry and Sarah wanted to know exactly what had been going on in their absence. Rowan slumped into an armchair with his claws dangling listlessly.

"What were you all thinking?" Aunt Sarah yelled at them, her eyes wildly roaming all over them. She was torn between concern and rage as she paced in front of Charity, Nora and Alfie, who were huddled together on the sofa. "Why on *earth* would a group of children think the best plan of action is to take on *criminals* themselves? *Anything* could have happened! You all could have been hurt…or worse!" Sarah's hands jerked upwards as if she was throwing confetti over them. "And you!" She pointed at Alfie. "We left you in charge! You were meant to be looking after these two. We thought we could trust you." Her eyes were now glistening with tears.

"Mum…" Nora tried to explain but she was cut off.

"Don't *Mum* me! Telling me you couldn't come because you had homework to do. All lies! You're grounded, all of you! I –"

"Here love. Take this and sit down. Let them get a word in." Uncle Henry handed his wife a cup of tea and indicated for her to take a seat. "I'd love to hear what they've got to say for themselves."

Sarah huffed but took the tea and sat down. Uncle Henry remained standing in the doorway like a statue. "Let's hear it then," he commanded.

Charity, Nora and Alfie looked at each other, unsure where to start.

"We weren't going out to lie in wait for some unknown criminals," Alfie began, tentatively, shooting quick looks at both his parents. "We knew who it was going to be."

"Oh, for goodness sake! How could you *possibly* have known who it was going to be?" Aunt Sarah interrupted, nearly spilling her tea.

"Charity worked it out," Nora supplied.

"Is that true Charity?" Uncle Henry asked wearily, slouching against the door frame, as if he needed its support to remain standing.

"Err…yeah…"

"Can I ask how? How could you have possibly known that your parents, my own brother, was doing this to us? Uncle Henry plonked himself heavily into an armchair, afraid his legs might give way if he remained standing any longer.

"Well..." Charity began. And then the whole story poured out: how she had put the pieces together to work out the identity of the farm's enemies. "It was mainly the ring." Charity said, focussing on a stain on the carpet, unable to meet anyone's eyes. "It bugged me as I knew I'd seen it before. I even dreamt about it. Then, recently when I was going through the photos on my phone, I saw it. I zoomed in to be sure as I didn't want to believe it, but it's quite a distinctive ring. And there it was…on my mother's finger. She's got so much jewellery, she doesn't wear the same things all the time, so that's why I didn't immediately realise it was hers, but once I saw that picture, I remembered. And then it made sense how she told me not to show anyone the ring and how it went missing from my sock drawer.

"And then I thought of other things, like how they hardly ever reply to my text messages or show me any attention what-so-ever, but as soon as I came here, they were suddenly always in touch, interested in what was going on. That's how I knew. They didn't send me here so that I'd have a nice summer with you guys, they sent me here so I could be their spy and let them know what was happening here. *Not that I knew I was here for that!*" Charity looked at everyone, panicked. "I'd never have said a word to them if I'd known what they were doing." She dropped her eyes back to the carpet stain. "I just don't get it. Why would they do this?" she whispered.

Uncle Henry dragged a hand over his stubble, creating a rasping sound that cut through the silence. "We don't blame you Charity. Of course we don't…and I don't understand it either. It makes no sense."

"Well, I'm sure we'll find out tomorrow, since we didn't get to hear the explanation tonight. It's been a long day and I think everyone needs to get to bed. So come on, up you go." Aunt Sarah chivvied everyone up briskly, scooping a fast-asleep Rowan up and carrying him upstairs. Charity, Nora and Alfie pretended to go into their rooms but when they heard the stairs creak as Aunt Sarah descended, they were all of the same mind and sneaked back out again. Sitting on the landing, they strained to hear the conversation taking place downstairs. Fortunately, Aunt Sarah hadn't closed the living room door so they could hear most of what was said.

"...jealousy...what else could it be?"

"...took it badly when Dad left the farm to me but he got money. It's not like he got nothing...what's there to be jealous of?"

"...changed when he met her...probably her doing...never happy...always wanting more."

"But how could making us lose the farm benefit them in any way?"

"...thought they'd get a share of the sale price? Who knows?"

The voices soon dropped to low mutterings and the three eavesdroppers could no longer make out their words. Alfie signalled that he was calling it a night and crept off to his room. Nora gave Charity a tight hug before they too headed to bed.

***

The next morning Charity lay, tangled in her sheets, dreading the day ahead. Her arm still hurt her and her brain felt like a computer that was about to overheat. She hadn't had a moment's sleep and her soggy pillow made her hair stick to her face. She dragged herself to the bathroom and showered, then spent the rest of the morning mooching around restlessly waiting for news.

Eventually, there was a knock at the door and the police officer from the previous evening was shown into the kitchen.

"Good afternoon, Mr and Mrs Glenn," he said. "I'm afraid the other Mr and Mrs Glenn have denied all charges against them. I know there is the video footage…" he glanced at Nora who had been about to protest, "but I'm afraid it's quite dark and blurry. There are no clear shots of their faces to establish their involvement, so I'm not sure it would stand up in court."

He waited for a reaction but the family in front of him just stared, dumbfounded. This clearly wasn't the news they'd been expecting.

"Mr Glenn has an…offer for you. He's said that if you drop the charges against him and his wife, he will pay for the damage. Not that he's actually admitting to causing it." Still, nobody spoke. "It might be for the best. There's no proof that any of what happened was down to them, so accepting his offer would give you some satisfaction."

He stood up to leave just as Gwen ambled into the kitchen through the open door. She carried a Transformer in her mouth. It looked like Optimus Prime.

"I'll…err…leave it with you. Have a think and get back to me. Let me know what you decide." He wrote down a phone number on the corner of a newspaper lying on the kitchen table and squeezed out, past Gwen.

***

The rest of August passed by quickly and September was soon approaching. Charity was outside sweeping the yard with her cousins when they heard a car pull up. Straightening up and shielding her eyes from the sun, Charity saw it was her father's car. He was in the driver's seat but there was no sign of her mother.

The car door closed with a thud and Charity's dad stood awkwardly beside it.

"Charity, love. I've come to get you. I know you haven't wanted to speak to me, but it's time to come home now."

Charity gripped the handle of her sweeping brush tightly but didn't reply. She could feel her cousins' eyes on her, watching to see how she'd react. She had blanked all of her father's text messages and refused to speak to him on the phone since their release. There had been no contact from her mother.

"Come on, love. Chloe will be home soon. What will we tell her if you're not there? Come home for your sister," he pleaded.

"Where's Mum?" Charity's voice was sharp. "Too busy to come? Or she doesn't want to show her face here?"

"Mum's...well...look, Charity, school starts next week so you've got to come back. Now go and get your things and let's go, okay?" He looked around nervously. Charity wondered whether he was more nervous about seeing his brother or taking on Guieseppe for round two. She was obviously nearby as they all heard an angry honk.

"I'm not going with you."

"Aww Charity, now stop –"

"No, you stop!" Charity flung down her broom and strode towards her father. "Stop pretending like nothing's happened! You were caught red-handed. On the night, you were going to explain, but then, the next day, you denied having anything to do with any of it. Why? I bet Mum talked you out of it. She wouldn't want it all to come out and damage her reputation, would she? If only I hadn't called the police. She wouldn't've had the chance to change your mind. But we all know you're lying, or why else would you offer to pay for all the damage?" Charity didn't pause for breath. All her pent up feelings fired the words from her like bullets. "You've never apologised to me for using me, never explained to Uncle Henry why you did this. I'm not coming home to that toxic house. I'm staying here where people actually know who I am and like me. Aunt Sarah has enrolled me to start at Nora's school and I can't wait so…so…*go away*. And if Chloe comes back and wonders where I am, you can just tell her. And tell her why too."

"Charity, look, it isn't what you think. Mum and I weren't involved in all that stuff that went on at the farm. We…"

"I know what I saw, Dad. You were both there to wreck the quad bike, and I found Mum's ring in the tool shed the day it was vandalised. You're lying, and we all know it."

Shaking, Charity's eyes and throat burned with the tears she fought to hold back. Fearing that they would break free and betray her, she ducked her head and ran towards the house.

Her father had been about to follow her but stopped when he spotted Guieseppe the guard goose rounding a corner, swaggering into the yard like a gangster looking for trouble. He yelped as if he'd been electrocuted and jumped in his car, slamming the door just in time. The car reversed back out of the yard, followed by Guieseppe flapping her giant white wings. As the car drove away, she ruffled her feathers and waggled her tail as if to say 'good riddance' and resumed her patrol.

Alfie, Rowan and Nora found Charity leaning against the kitchen cupboards when they followed her into the house. She was still shaking and her eyes were red. No-one knew what to say to her, even Rowan.

"This calls for chocolate," Nora announced, awkwardly. "Let's see what we've got."

They all followed her into the kitchen and sat down while she raided the goodies tin. "Just Kit

Kats I'm afraid," she said, passing one to everyone.

They sat quietly for a few seconds before a crunching sound broke the silence. They all stared at Alfie, who had just unwrapped his bar and bitten straight into it.

"WHAT ARE YOU DOING?" Demanded Nora, looking at Alfie like he was eating his own snot.

"Wo-oo-meem?" he replied, halfway through munching his chocolate.

"Why are you eating your Kit Kat like that?" Nora said. "That's not the right way to eat it. Everyone knows you have to *SNAP IT IN HALF!"*

"Ders no wrob ay do ea ah Kit Kat." Alfie said, his mouth once again full.

"Er, yes there is," said Nora, placing her hands on her hips. "And that's it." She pointed accusingly at Alfie eating his Kit Kat as a whole bar.

"Nahhhh," Alfie replied before swallowing. "There's no Kit Kat God who says 'thou shalt snap a Kit Kat before consuming it."

"No but it's widely known that the whole point of a Kit Kat is to snap it in half before eating it," Rowan joined in. And then you nibble the chocolate off the sides and ends before eating the wafer bits."

"No you don't!" Nora and Alfie cried in unison, both apparently horrified by this additional how-to-eat-a Kit Kat method.

"Charity, what do you think?" Nora looked to her cousin, including her in their debate.

Charity looked between the three of them, and rolled her eyes. In the midst of her life falling apart, here they were arguing about how to eat a Kit Kat. But she knew what they were doing: trying to cheer her up and take her mind off what had just happened. They were so daft, yet she loved them so much, despite her short amount of time living with them. The fact that they noticed her, understood her, and treated her like one of the family, meant so much.

She had turned her back on her parents, and whenever she thought about it, she found herself biting her fingernails down to the quick. But against this loss, was the realisation that she still had family and people who cared for her. She already felt more at home here than she ever had at 'home.' This was where she was meant to be.

From: Charity Glenn <cg1471@hotmail.co.uk>
To: Richard Glenn <rjglenn@gmail.com>
Subject: My news

Dear Mum and Dad,

Haven't heard from you for a while, which is disappointing, but if you're not going to admit to what you did and make up for it, I don't want to hear from you. I thought you might like to know what I've been up to though, so here's my news.

My new school is great. I'm in Year 8 and I've been put in a form with Nora, so I'm in a lot of classes with her too. I'm doing well and have joined the orienteering club, which is interesting and different. We've been doing some work in Personal Development about careers. It's got me thinking about my future. My cousins all know exactly what they want to do: Nora either wants to work for the R.S.P.C.A or be a vet, Alfie wants to farm and Rowan, of course, is already in training to be an actor. I've never had any idea about what I might want to do, but now I'm thinking about the police. I think I'd make a good detective and it would be a rewarding job to catch criminals and bring justice to the victims of crime. Don't you think?

My room here has been redecorated and it's all nice and tidy. It's great living here, as part of a family where people all take an interest in each other's lives. It's not just a house, it's a home. Things are looking up on the farm. Apparently, the silage crop was good and they're hoping to get another cut too, so they'll be all set up for winter. And Aunt Sarah has set up a farm shop, selling eggs, vegetables and cakes for now, though she's hoping to expand and do homemade bread, goat's cheese and jams soon. Nora and I help out quite a bit and she's getting lots of customers from the village and new housing estate, now that people are moving in. They love Guieseppe's huge eggs - they're a best seller. Even Mr Reekworth is a customer! Everyone is keen to support the farm and the family, I think, now they know about the sabotage. There's a really nice community feeling now.

Chloe's been in touch to ask why I'm here and not at home. I assume you've probably told her a completely untrue version of events but I've filled her in on what really happened. Not sure if she'll believe me, since she's your favourite, but we'll see.

I feel sorry for you two. You have a wonderful family here that you're missing out on, and we still don't know why. I may forgive you in the future, but only if you earn it. If you choose to accept this challenge, you need to apologise properly to Uncle Henry and explain why you did it. Give him the final piece to solve the puzzle of Hazel Tree Farm. You owe him that much. Maybe then we can start to put this family back together.

Anyway, Rowan has just arrived in my room riding a dragon, so he says, to tell me that tea is ready. He appears to have no control of his dragon as it's just thrown him off and he's now drowning in my carpet which is really the Sea of Doom. Who knew? I'd better go and rescue him before he pegs it.

You know where we are if you decide to do the right thing.

Your daughter,

Charity x

AUTHOR'S NOTE

Spoiler alert! Don't read this part until you've read the story. There's a reason this is at the back of the book!

K.S. Aitken is the pen name for a group of people who were all involved in the production of this book through the Keswick School Writers & Illustrators Club. Here they are:

Writers: Erin Wallace, Niamh McMullin, Annabelle Brett, Ellie Turnbull, Amanda Maley, Elizabeth Murphy, Laura Turnbull, Phoebe Hankin, Isabella Hankin, Leanna Thompson

Editors: Martha Wiseman, Ben Page, Marianne Hodgson, Abbie Wilkins, Samuel Christian

Illustrators: Ella Armstrong, Abbie Wilkins, Emily Haddath, Katie Treble, Janie Diamond (with thanks to artist, Paul Wilmott)

Helen Robinson: all of the above!

This story took two years to complete from start to finish. From the early ideas stage to planning the story, through the long months of actually writing and illustrating it, to the final stages of editing and proofreading. It's been a long road but the team remained dedicated and committed, turning up every week to do the hard work. It's funny that no-one was keen to do a farming story in the beginning, but the way they collaborated on the development of the story to make it dark, mysterious and funny, all at the same time, meant that they all came to love it.

The idea for this story came from the fact that there are many students in our school who belong to the farming community. They are always looking for books related to farming in the library, but there isn't much in the way of fiction. So, we decided to write a book for them. But, as no-one in the club knew anything about farming, we needed to do some research. We also knew that the story needed to be of interest to readers outside the farming community too.

So, we headed off, by kind invitation of Chris and Judith Wilson, to their farm: Skirwith Hall Farm, near Penrith. There we received a full farm tour, meeting the animals, machinery and people that make up a dairy farm. Armed with all the photos we took, the answers to our questions, and notes taken on the tour, we headed back to school to come up with the outline for a mystery story set on a farm that would explore family tensions.

And that was that. We were off. The writers would meet weekly to work on a chapter. They worked in two groups, both writing the same chapter. When the chapters were complete, they were sent off to local primary schools, Borrowdale and Braithwaite, who read them and gave us feedback on their thoughts on the two versions of the same chapter. The editors would then use the feedback to combine the best elements from both groups before the writers met again to hear the edited chapter read aloud, discuss what would happen next and set off to repeat the process. Meanwhile the illustrators worked with artist, Paul Wilmott, to find an illustration style for the book that they could all use to unify the pictures being produced by five different people.

And that's how it continued for around 18 months. Until the school was forced to close due to the Coronavirus just before the project was completed. The story was finished with the aid of Google Classroom to allow us to share ideas of how we wanted it to end. It was then edited again, several times, by Amanda Horan at Let's Get Booked (who also designed the amazing cover for the book), and read by a number of beta readers.

We hope that you enjoyed the story. We know that there is some divided opinion about the ending and whether or not the reasons behind the actions of the culprits should have been revealed. We discussed it at length and decided that it would probably be somewhat dull for young readers to hear all about the business and financial reasoning for their behaviour. Rather than explaining it in detail, which we felt would slow the story down, we opted to give hints and clues to let the reader come to their own conclusions about why they might have done what they did. We chose to solve one part of the mystery: who was behind the incidents on the farm, but to leave the reasoning for the reader to wonder about. We thought an ending where not everything is happy and resolved felt more realistic and truer to life.

As for consequences and justice at the end, this was something else we discussed in detail. Should we have sent the culprits to prison? Is it disappointing that they 'got away with it'? For us, we felt we didn't want to have a happy ending but we did want an ending with some hope in it. The consequence is the loss of their relationship with their family. But Charity shows them that the door is open for forgiveness and reconciliation, if they do the right thing by owning up and explaining their actions. We hope that this is a positive message to end the story on and that it creates an opportunity for thought, debate and discussion.

We'd like to thank everyone who helped us and got involved with this project. It's been difficult but also a lot of fun and a unique experience. Final thanks goes to Elterwater Press, our sponsor and publisher for giving us this opportunity.

Printed in Great Britain
by Amazon

50003489R00097